Strateg
Air Command
1946–92
"Peace is Our Profession"

KEVIN WRIGHT

Front cover image: From 1966 to 1989, the Mach 3+ SR-71A Blackbird was the pride of SAC's manned airborne reconnaissance capability. (USAF)

Title page image: An SAC B-52H, Cold War strategic bomber and Cold War icon, now in service for over 60 years. (USAF/SSgt Bill Thompson)

Contents page image: SAC HQ at Offutt Air Force Base (AFB) in the 1980s. (USAF/SSgt Scott Stewart)

Back cover image: A B-52 crew runs toward an alert aircraft. Fully armed with nuclear weapons, crews did not know if it was a practice or the real thing. (USAF/MSgt Bob Wickley)

Published by Key Books
An imprint of Key Publishing Ltd
PO Box 100
Stamford
Lincs PE9 1XQ

www.keypublishing.com

The right of Kevin Wright to be identified as the author of this book has been asserted in accordance with the Copyright, Designs and Patents Act 1988 Sections 77 and 78.

Copyright © Kevin Wright, 2023

ISBN 978 1 80282 257 1

Typeset by SJmagic DESIGN SERVICES, India.

Contents

Chapter 1   Wartime Leftovers and Early Strategy 4

Chapter 2   Turbulent Growth...10

Chapter 3   SAC's Tanker Force 21

Chapter 4   New Bombers...25

Chapter 5   Life in SAC 37

Chapter 6   Missile Forces..43

Chapter 7   Crisis and War..52

Chapter 8   New Aircraft and Missiles 58

Chapter 9   "SAC Recon"...67

Chapter 10   Command, Control, Communications 74

Chapter 11   Declining Cold War and Sudden Hot War 82

Chapter 12   Closing SAC, but Remaining Strategic 93

Chapter 1

Wartime Leftovers and Early Strategy

From its formation in 1946 to its demise in 1992, Strategic Air Command (SAC) was the most visible element of the US nuclear triad. During SAC's formative years, from 1948 to 1957, it was dominated by two giant characters, General Curtis LeMay and vice commander General Thomas Power, who succeeded him. In those early years, SAC grew from operating World War Two B-29 bombers to having a global presence, controlling a huge arsenal of nuclear weapons and capable of rapidly projecting US power around the world.

When SAC was created on March 21, 1946, General George Kenney became SAC's first commanding general. The tasks facing him were considerable. US nuclear doctrine was ill defined, initially regarding them as just large, conventional high-explosive weapons. A viable bomber force had to be created from existing equipment, at a time when the US military was rapidly demobilizing its personnel and largely in a state of neglect. No definable concept of "nuclear strategy" existed as President Truman, the US government, military, and nuclear scientific communities struggled to come to terms with the immense power of these new weapons. However, that task was soon shaped by events emanating from Moscow. The creation of the "Iron Curtain" in Eastern Europe, the detonation of the first Soviet nuclear weapon in 1949, a new communist regime in China, and soon the Korean War all helped focus US defense and foreign policy. Its primary goal was to contain an expansive Soviet Union.

In 1947, SAC's nuclear bomber capability was solely reliant on 32 of 65 modified World War Two "Silverplate" B-29s adapted in readiness to drop nuclear weapons on Japan. The US nuclear stockpile was tiny in comparison to what it later became and even the few available weapons not in US military custody, the nuclear "cores," were separately held by the US Atomic Energy Commission. In an

During World War Two, 65 B-29s received "Silverplate" modifications to carry nuclear weapons. One was a B-29A "Bockscar" that dropped its "Fat Man" atomic bomb on Nagasaki. (NMUSAF)

emergency, the cores would have been fitted into the early weapons and then transported overseas for use by forward-based B-29s. This process was measured in days and weeks, rather than the minutes and hours that became associated with later Cold War crises. SAC battled to gain full control of the nuclear weapon cores but did not do so until 1956.

SAC's main targets were initially Soviet cities; however, its B-29s did not have the range to hit targets in the USSR directly from the US. Overseas forward basing was essential to hit targets in Eastern Europe and western Russia. SAC re-evaluated its target list after the detonation of the first Soviet nuclear weapon in August 1949. It became concerned about the possibilities of a pre-emptive attack on its forward airfields in Britain that would house its nuclear-capable bombers. The British had similar concerns about a possible surprise attack on the SAC bases and its own nascent nuclear V-bomber force, then nearing service entry. Accordingly, it strengthened Royal Air Force (RAF) fighter defenses to protect those nuclear bases and the British mainland. To stop the Soviet bombers, SAC adopted a pre-emptive strike plan to hit the airfields from where their nuclear-capable TU-4s (themselves reverse-engineered B-29s) would be launched. The many airfields available to the Soviet Air Force meant SAC adopted a much more extensive target list and required a corresponding increase in aircraft and atomic weapons.

SAC was soon permitted to rotate its nuclear forces through periods of temporary duty at British bases, including this B-36 at RAF Lakenheath in 1951. (USAF)

The first Soviet nuclear bomber was the TU-4, reverse engineered from the US B-29. (Kevin Wright)

From the early 1950s, nuclear strategy developed into a new discipline, which became a major strand of US foreign and defense policy. RAND Corporation analyst and academic Albert Wohlstetter and his colleagues, Fred Hoffman, Robert Lutz, and Henry Rowen among others, were instrumental in outlining the different options for the basing and operation of US nuclear forces. Two particular studies: The *Selection and Use of Strategic Air Bases* (1954) and *Protecting US Power to Strike Back in the 1950s and 1960s* (1956) proved particularly influential in SAC's organizational and operational evolution.

The first concluded that SAC bomber forces should be largely based in the continental US, because overseas bases were too vulnerable, although they had possibilities as forward bases for air-refueling assets and recovering bombers. However, US basing required far better early warning and the dispersal of bomber forces within the US. The second study addressed the vulnerability of US nuclear forces to a surprise attack as Soviet capabilities developed, reinforcing the first study. In addition, recommendations suggested the US's early warning radar systems and air defenses be greatly expanded and SAC aircraft become well practiced at dispersed operations. Such changes would necessitate greatly enhanced communications and command and control capacities. Finally, it suggested that key facilities be hardened to protect the nuclear bombers, missiles, and personnel, to ensure a viable second-strike capability was still available after an enemy attack. Many of the conclusions of these two studies soon became built into SAC strategy, its daily training, operations, and war plans that would persist into the 1990s.

The above-ground SAC HQ administration building in 1958, connected to the below-ground hardened command center. (USAF)

Above: Pre-computerization inside the SAC command post, large wall displays were used to display aircraft movements and readiness status. (USAF)

Right: By February 1961 SAC's underground command post had its own TV system to distribute important information to SAC commanders. (USAF)

As the Cold War deepened, US public fears and, at times, near hysteria in Congress about Soviet nuclear capabilities saw a bonanza for the advanced technology defense companies. This fed through operationally to a large proportion of the additional defense resources being channeled toward SAC. It provided funding for new aircraft, new bombs, new bases, numerous ballistic missile programs, the design and construction of a vast early warning radar system, a greatly enhanced command and control network, and significantly improved continental air defenses.

SAC's first war-fighting task came when its B-29s were committed to conventional strategic bombing operations over Korea, following the North's invasion of the South on June 25, 1950. By mid-August B-29s from the 19th Bomb Group, 22nd, 92nd, 98th, and 307th Bomb Wings, based in Japan, were committed to the conflict, mounting mass conventional bombing missions over industrial targets and population centers. By the time a ceasefire came into force on July 27, 1953, B-29s had flown more than 21,000 sorties and dropped 167,000 tons of bombs. In total, 34 aircraft were lost, 16 to fighters, four to flak, and 14 through accidents.

Modeled on oil rigs, three of five planned "Texas Towers" built provided radar coverage to the US Eastern Seaboard. (USAF)

The Distant Early Warning radar at Foymount in Ontario. Similar "pine tree line" radar stations were built close to the US border across Canada, parts of Alaska, and the Aleutian Islands in the 1950s. (Department of National Defense)

During the Korean War, SAC B-29s dropped more than 600,000 tons of bombs on enemy cities and positions. (USAF)

Chapter 2

Turbulent Growth

G eneral LeMay became SAC's commander in October 1948, remaining in charge until the end of June 1957. His vice commander was Gen Power, from October 1948 until April 1954. After a brief period as Head of Air Research and Development Command, Power returned to Offutt Air Force Base (AFB) as SAC commander, replacing LeMay who became United States Air Force (USAF) Vice Chief of Staff in July 1957. Power remained head of SAC until November 30, 1964. Holding the two most senior posts for more than 16 years between them, they shaped SAC's structure, organization, and ethos – much of which has persisted beyond the demise of SAC itself. Of SAC's 13 commanders in its 46-year existence, LeMay and Power were in charge for more than one-third of that time.

Both men were regarded as disciplinarians, with perceived infractions and failures taken very seriously. During 1949 LeMay was given the power to award "spot promotions" to bomber crew officers if they performed exceptionally well. "Spots" were later authorized for enlisted crew members too. The promotions were "real" in that crew members received the pay and rank badges of the higher grade, but they were still considered only temporary. They reverted to their previous rank on leaving their crew, or if they were later rated as deficient in any of the many operational evaluations SAC crews were

Above left: In charge from 1948 to 1957, the charismatic General Curtis LeMay was SAC's second and best-known commander. (NARA)

Above right: General Thomas Power was SAC's third commander from 1957 to 1964. He oversaw the integration of SAC's InterContinental Ballistic Missile (ICBM) force and established the Joint Strategic Target Planning Staff (JSTPS) that decided targeting priorities. (USAF)

exposed to. Spot promotions were intended as motivation and morale boosters for elite crews; however, others in the air force saw it as a divisive program and it was eventually halted.

B-36 Peacemaker

If the term "leviathan" can ever be applied to an aircraft, it must surely be to Convair's giant B-36 "Peacemaker." Conceived in 1941 as a possible transatlantic bomber in case Great Britain was overrun by the Nazis, it did not make its first flight until August 8, 1946. Initially powered by six propellers, with four jet engines added later, it had a 230ft wingspan, was 163ft long, and sat 46ft high at the tail. Entering service in 1948, a total of 383 aircraft were built including bomber, reconnaissance, and several experimental versions.

Film star James Stewart, a distinguished wartime bomber pilot and later Air Force Reserve brigadier general, who became SAC's Deputy Director of Operations, took the lead role in the Hollywood film *Strategic Air Command*. While not having the most engaging plot, it has visually spectacular aerial

Above: As big as the Boeing B-29 was, it was dwarfed by the giant Convair B-36 Peacemaker. (USAF)

Below left: The B-36 was already outdated as it entered service. Getting its six propellor and four jet engines "turning and burning" was a major achievement. (USAF)

Below right: To reach the rear of the B-36, crew members had to pull themselves along on a trolley, down a tunnel that ran along much of the aircraft. (USAF via AAHS)

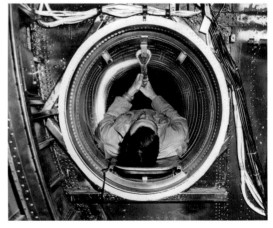

The NB-36H investigated the feasibility of nuclear-powered aircraft. For 18 months, from September 17, 1955, it completed 215 hours of flight time, with the reactor running for 89 hours, although it did not power it. (USAF)

sequences of the B-36. The aircraft carried a crew of 15, but was not very highly thought of by most, who regarded it as difficult to operate. It was slow, hard to maneuver, and its 40,000ft cruising altitude was relatively easily reached by fighters of the time. Its World War Two technology was very rapidly outdated by advances in aerodynamics and engine design, with the last of these vast beasts retiring in 1959.

Boeing B-50 Superfortress

First flying in 1947, the B-50 was a modest development of the B-29A and fitted with more powerful Pratt & Whitney R-4360 engines. Some 370 were eventually built and equipped five SAC wings. The first were delivered in 1948 and completed with the formation of the 97th Bombardment Wing (BW) in December 1950. By 1953 they were being replaced by early B-47s. A significant number were converted to reconnaissance (RB-50), tanker (KB-50), and weather reconnaissance (WB-50) versions that saw a much longer service life. The KB-50 and WB-50 versions soldiered on into the 1960s.

The B-50D differed little from its B-29 predecessor but had more powerful engines. (USAF)

B-50Ds had a good service record but only saw frontline service for a few years, replaced by the B-47. (AAHS E Stoltz collection)

Boeing B-47 Stratojet

An early icon of SAC was the Boeing B-47. Developed toward the end of the war, two prototypes were ordered in 1946, with the first flying in December 1947. A cutting-edge design, with thin swept wings and powered by six engines, the B-47 entered service in 1951. It became the mainstay of SAC's medium bomber force, with some 2,042 produced up to fall 1956. At the B-47's peak, it equipped 28 bomber wings. Specialist variants were operated in photo-reconnaissance and signals intelligence roles that equipped five wings. Production of 399 B-47Bs was followed by 1,341 definitive B-47Es. Another 240 airframes were produced as RB-47Es and 32 as RB-47H/ERB-47H. Many B-47s were later converted to other specialist tasks, such as weather reconnaissance and test roles.

B-47s as far as the eye can see on the assembly line in Wichita, Kansas, where production B-47s were assembled. (AAHS/NARA)

RB-47Hs flew peripheral reconnaissance missions skirting Soviet territory, collecting signals intelligence. (NMUSAF)

The B-47 was always hampered by its relatively short range without aerial refueling, which necessitated significant overseas forward basing to maintain a credible nuclear retaliatory capability. "Reflex" operations would see small numbers of B-47s regularly rotated through seven forward bases in the UK, three in Spain, and another three in North Africa. There they sat on high readiness, fueled and armed for their war missions. Within the US a major dispersal plan even included the use of some civilian airports for wartime operations, a plan that was used during the Cuban Missile Crisis.

The B-47's importance had begun to decline after 1960, as the B-52 became available in significant numbers. The switch from high-level to low-level operations after 1960 imposed much greater fatigue on the B-47s airframes, which led to several losses and required a program to strengthen the aircraft's wing mountings. The final phase-out of B-47 bombers began in 1963 and was completed by 1965.

A B-47E from the 301st Bombardment Wing (BW) sits on "Reflex Alert" at RAF Brize Norton in August 1963. (AAHS/Jack Friel)

Lincoln Air Force Base (AFB), Nebraska, was home to the 98th and 307th BW B-47Es up to the mid-1960s. (Scott Haydon)

At their peak, 1,740 B-47B/Es bombers equipped 28 SAC medium bomber wings. (USAF)

B-47E 52-166 made the last ever B-47 flight on June 17, 1986. Having not flown for more than 20 years and sitting in the Mojave Desert, it was briefly restored to flying condition for a 43-minute ferry flight from the Naval Air Weapons Station at China Lake to Castle AFB to be put on public display. (USAF/TSgt Michael Haggerty)

The Single Integrated Operational Plan

The development of the target list for the growing stockpile of US nuclear weapons was an unsystematic one. Some planners favored hitting Russian cities, others striking bomber and, later, missile bases. SAC, US Navy and Army targeting priorities were developed separately and closely held within each service, with little to no co-ordination. Thus, three different plans developed that involved much duplication. SAC's 1955 strike plan envisaged the use of 155 bombers, mainly the comparatively new, yet short-range, B-47s. These had to be based with their nuclear weapons at vulnerable forward bases in the UK, Canada, Greenland, Spain, Morocco, Saudi Arabia, and Japan, if they were to be viable.

It was only in 1960, following the creation of the Joint Strategic Target Planning Staff at Omaha, that a more co-ordinated tri-service approach was developed. This eventually eliminated much of the duplication and brought about a more coherent targeting policy. The Single Integrated Operational Plan (SIOP) was not nuanced: the plan required a single, sequenced massive strike against the USSR. On receipt of a valid "go code," bombers and missiles would be launched to attack their preassigned targets; the whole plan would take from just over an hour for the first alert force missiles to strike, until it was completed 28 hours later. It was only after the Kennedy administration assumed office in 1961 that this and other linked problems began to be addressed. However, SIOP did not really evolve into a more flexible form until the late 1970s, under President Jimmy Carter.

The infamous "red telephone" in the SAC command post gave the senior controller near instantaneous voice contact with SAC units across the world. (USAF)

A 1967 alert line of B-52s fitted with AGM-28 Hound Dog missiles. Intended as a temporary weapon, it remained in service for 15 years. (USAF)

High flying, a B-52 leaves its distinctive smoky trail during a *Red Flag* training exercise. (USAF/SSgt Vernon Young)

SAC FIGHTER FORCE AND "FICON"

From 1946 to 1960, SAC had its own fighter force, which reached seven wings at its peak. It used a wide range of fighters as bomber escorts, but as the SAC bomber force modernized, these fighters were no longer able to keep up with them. Types operated included P-47s, P-51s, P-80s, F-82s, F-84s, F-86s, and F-101s. The force reached its pinnacle in 1955, with 554 aircraft of several versions assigned to it.

Briefly from 1957, SAC operated F-101As, assigned to the 27th Fighter Wing and originally envisaged as escort fighters, the F-101's design got overtaken by other developments and switched to the tactical nuclear role, carrying a single weapon. The F-101, however, did not have the range required to strike deep into Soviet territory, and so the wing was soon re-assigned to Tactical Air Command (TAC).

The 27th Fighter Group (FG) was the only SAC unit to operate F-82E Twin Mustangs. Between 1947 and 1950, they flew fighter escort operations for its bombers. (NARA)

Right: The SAC escort fighter force reached its peak around 1955, flying 554 aircraft including F-84Gs from the 31st and 508th Strategic Fighter Wings. (USAF)

Below: Described as a "floating wing tip," Project Tip Tow used two specially modified EF-84Ds and a B-29 to explore ways of extending the escort fighters range for SAC bombers. (USAF)

Other, more exotic ideas emerged to extend the range of escort fighters and provide the bombers with their own escort. Project Tip Tow was described as a "floating wing tip" concept, that saw two F-84s attached to the wing tip of a B-29. After take-off, all three aircraft would join up and connect together and the B-29 effectively carried the load of all three aircraft. The difficulty was that each of the three aircraft still had to be manually flown and, almost inevitably, on April 24, 1953, when one of the F-84s developed a control surface fault, it collided with the B-29, causing both to fatally crash.

Another idea from Convair was the Project Tom Tom FICON (Fighter Conveyor) concept – an attempt to carry a "parasite fighter" attached to a special compartment built into the underside of an adapted B-36. After testing, the system saw limited service with SAC in 1955–56. Using ten modified GRB-36D carriers from the 99th Strategic Reconnaissance Wing (SRW), they worked with 25 modified RF-84Ks from the 91st Strategic Reconnaissance Squadron (SRS). While the idea ostensibly worked, it was challenging even for experienced test pilots in ideal conditions, with several RF-84Ks damaged in training flights. In more realistic operational situations, with less experienced pilots, it would probably have proved next to useless and was quickly abandoned in April 1956.

The parasite fighter concept saw an F-84 attached to the underside of its GRB-36D host. Launch required the F-84 to be lowered by a special "trapeze" and released. (USAF)

Chapter 3

SAC's Tanker Force

S AC was a pioneer of the aerial refueling techniques that became so essential to its Cold War mission. First were the KB-29Ms, which utilized a probe and drogue refueling system on 92 converted B-29As and B-29Bs, for the 43rd and 509th Aerial Refueling Squadrons from 1949. However, this system proved too slow and unreliable for SAC, which opted instead for Boeing's "flying boom" system used ever since. This was first used by 116 B-29s, which became KB-29Ps in 1950–51. After briefly serving as bombers, 112 B-50D airframes were converted, mostly into KB-50Js, and 24 TB-50H trainers were converted into KB-50Ks, with the first of these delivered in January 1958. Gradually phased out from 1964 onwards, some of the B-50 fuel-pumping equipment and external jet pods were transferred on to its successor, the KC-97.

Boeing's KC-97 Stratofreighter, modified from the original C-97 transport, was another derivative of the B-29 Superfortress. Work began on the new type before the end of World War Two and between

Above: A KB-29 refuels a B-29. SAC opted for the boom method of aerial refueling able to transfer greater amounts of fuel at higher speed than hose options. (USAF)

Right: SAC's 91st SRW was the first equipped with an RB-45C Tornado and flew reconnaissance missions during the Korean War, supported by the wing's KB-29P tankers. (USAF)

1944 and 1958, 888 C-97s were built in numerous versions, 811 of them becoming KC-97 tankers. While an advance over the KB-29s, the KC-97s slow speed and altitude limits made it unsuitable for SAC's new generation of faster, higher-flying jet bombers, particularly the B-52.

The Boeing KC-135A became the mainstay of SAC's aerial-refueling force from the late 1950s, with some 820 aircraft purchased between 1955 and 1964 as SAC had become the sole USAF provider for aerial refueling. Most of the airframes were assigned to SAC in their early days, with 732 used as tankers and the remainder operated as transports, airborne command posts, reconnaissance platforms, VIP transport, and research aircraft. Capable of long endurance and able to keep pace with the bombers, the new KC-135A was an essential replacement for the struggling KC-97s. In the early years the demand for KC-135s for SIOP alert duty significantly outweighed their availability, with some crews having to maintain up to three weeks of every month on alert and so did little other flying.

However, SAC-owned tankers were not only used in support of SIOP and its own commitments, but also by the thirsty fleets of TAC and USAF commands in Europe and the Pacific. Later, the demands of the wars in South East Asia also depleted the availability of tankers for SIOP. From 1974, 128 KC-135As were gradually transferred to Air National Guard and Air Force Reserve units to mainly help meet the continuing non-SAC air-refueling demands.

A KC-97 refuels an RB-47. The KC-97 flew too slowly for the much faster B-47, which had to refuel at close to its stall speed. (USAF)

The KC-135A was a huge advance in aerial refueling capability, able to fly at similar speeds to the B-47 and B-52. (USAF)

A 28th BW KC-135A departs Ellsworth AFB, South Dakota, to refuel B-52s during Exercise *Global Shield '84*. (USAF/ TSgt Boyd Belcher)

KC-135As assigned for temporary duty with the 376th Strategic Wing (SW) at Kadena AFB, Japan, in 1988, working with the USAF Pacific Air Force. (USAF/TSgt Donald McMichael)

Chapter 4

New Bombers

The B-52 is the longest-serving US strategic bomber of all time; now flying for more than 70 years. Even the youngest airframes still in service are more than 60 years old and a replacement engine program, promised for more than 40 years, is only just getting underway in 2023. It can haul ordnance over vast distances, has flown around the world on non-stop missions and has taken part in every major US conflict since Vietnam. During its career, the B-52 has maintained long periods of continuous airborne and ground alert. It has flown mass conventional bombing, maritime reconnaissance missions, and launched standoff and other precision munitions.

The prototype XB-52 rolled out of Boeing's Seattle plant in considerable secrecy on November 29, 1951. During early ground testing, a partial failure of the pneumatic system caused widespread damage to the rear of one wing. As a result the second prototype, designated as a YB-52, became the first to fly on April 15, 1952. The XB-52's original tandem seating design was changed to a side-by-side arrangement for the YB-52.

Although having a gigantic 185ft wingspan with a huge 4,000sq ft area, the B-52's wing is very thin and flexible, with an incredible 32ft range of vertical movement at the tips. As a result, wing icing has rarely been a problem, with the constant wing flexing preventing significant ice accumulations. Its eight engines are pod mounted in pairs. The 159ft fuselage is essentially a long, thin, low-drag tube that contains a 28ft-long by 6ft-wide bomb bay. Another of the B-52's more unusual design features is its undercarriage. Outriggers protect the flexible wings, but the main landing gear can be turned up to 20 degrees on each side of the aircraft centerline. This permits "crab-like" landings in substantial crosswinds, where the wheels still point directly down the runway. In the early years, B-52 photos and film footage were careful not to reveal this innovative design feature.

The first production B-52A flew on August 5, 1954, with an order for 13 aircraft, which was reduced to just three, with the remainder becoming part of an enlarged order for 50 B-52Bs. The first arrived at Castle AFB on June 29, 1955. Twenty-seven aircraft were modified to become RB-52Bs, with

The first prototype, XB-52, had a tandem seat arrangement for its pilots. By the time the first YB-52 aircraft flew, it had the familiar side-by-side arrangement of the production aircraft. (Boeing)

Above left: The B-52s 28ft-long bomb bay could see it crammed with M117 conventional bombs or several nuclear weapons. (USAF)

Above right: Quietly disguised in early images of B-52s, by not showing it, was the aircraft's ability to "crab." The dual bicycle undercarriage enabled it to still align with the runway during heavy crosswind approaches. (USAF)

Below: The first production B-52A on its maiden flight from Boeing Field, August 5, 1954. (USAF)

The B-52D's rear armament consisted of four .50-caliber machine guns. (Kevin Wright)

the insertion of a two-man pressurized reconnaissance capsule into the bomb bay, which contained electronic listening and countermeasures equipment and had a photographic reconnaissance capability. Production soon switched to the B-52C variant, 35 of which were built, the first flying on March 9, 1956. Each new variant was powered by successive versions of the Pratt & Whitney J-57 engine. Defensive armament for the B-52A to F models was four 50-caliber tail-mounted machine guns housed in a radar-controlled turret, along with the operator.

The first large production run was for 170 B-52Ds. Assembly of the bomber was gradually switched from Boeing's Seattle plant to Wichita, with the first rolled out from the Kansas facility on December 7, 1955. The B-52D formed the mainstay of the Stratofortress fleet, with an increased emphasis on conventional rather than nuclear roles, until their retirement in 1983.

Externally identical to the B-52D, the first B-52E flew in October 1957 and was optimized for low-level operations with a much more sophisticated navigation capability. In service, its AN/ASQ-38 system was found to be less accurate and more difficult to maintain than promised, in particular its vital terrain-avoidance system required significant improvement. The B-52E was not deployed to South East Asia, with most removed from frontline service in 1967 and placed into storage between 1969 and 1970. Succeeded by the B-52F, which first flew on May 6, 1958, this model incorporated the more powerful J-57-P-43W engines. Using these engines required wing strengthening to accommodate the extra water tanks necessary for its fuel injection system. Externally differing very little from the B-52D, the final "F" model was delivered in February 1959. These initially experienced frequent fuel leaks at the interconnections between the aircraft's many wing tanks. Some were retired in 1967–68, but all went into storage during the latter half of 1978.

A B-52D in pre-South East Asia colors during routine SAC operations. (USAF)

B-52E 57-0161 from the 93rd BW at Castle AFB, California, in October 1967. (AAHS/Stephen Miller)

Final models

The B-52G and H versions were substantial developments over earlier models. The 193 B-52Gs built made it the most numerous variant, all delivered between November 1958 and February 1961. Crew comfort was improved, with pilots given better visibility, seating, and air conditioning alongside other minor changes. The most visible difference was a bigger, but 8ft shorter, tailfin. External fuel tanks were fitted, the wing's main rubber bladder tanks were replaced with integral ones, and the fuel management system was radically modified. The tail gunner's position was moved from isolation in the tail to join the rest of the crew, saving more than 1,000lb weight too. However, these modifications caused significant problems. The extra noise and vibration created by installing an engine water-injection system caused fatigue and cracking to the B-52G's flaps. The wing redesign and use of new aluminum alloys gave rise to fatigue cracks, exacerbated by constant low flying and extra airframe stresses during aerial refueling. This necessitated further wing redesign and replacement between 1961 and 1964. In the early 1980s, 98 B-52Gs were modified to carry the AGM-69B air-launched cruise missiles. Particularly valuable for maritime missions, external "heavy stores adapter beams" were fitted, which enabled the carriage of mines and harpoon anti-ship missiles.

The B-52H was the ultimate model of the giant bomber. Pratt & Whitney TF-33-P3 engines gave better thrust and fuel economy and allowed removal of the water-injection system, saving

A smoky, water injection induced take-off from RAF Marham by a 68th BW B-52G during a SAC–RAF bombing competition. (Chris Chennell)

Top: Ground crew members perform maintenance on a B-52G engine during Operation *Desert Shield*. (USAF/CMSgt Don Sutherland)

Above: A 456th BG B-52G armed with an AGM-28 Hound Dog nuclear missile. Operational from 1961 to 1976, it had more than a 750-mile range. (USAF)

Right: A 43rd Munitions Maintenance Squadron crew load Mk 52 training mines into a B-52G aircraft during Exercise *Team Spirit '85*. (USAF/ TSgt Boyd Belcher)

Above: A B-52 parked during *Pitch Black '84*, a joint US, Australian, and New Zealand exercise. (USAF/MSgt David N Craft)

Left: A Vulcan 20mm cannon mounted in the tail of a B-52H. (USAF/Sgt Vincent Kitts)

nearly 10,000lb in weight and removing the need to maintain large stocks of pre-positioned distilled water. Other improvements included replacing the rear machine guns with a single M-61 six-barrel 20mm gun and an improved fire control system.

Flying the huge aircraft at low level required better avionics and saw the installation of an AN/ASQ-151 "electro-optical viewing system" using Westinghouse low-light and Hughes Forward-Looking InfraRed (FLIR) sensors in the nose of both B-52Gs and H's from the early 1970s. This was connected to the terrain-avoidance radar, with its display visible at four positions in the aircraft. The vastly improved system immediately improved flight safety and gave the crews greater confidence to operate at low level. The last of the 742 B-52s bought for SAC was the 102nd "H" model delivered to Minot AFB on October 26, 1962.

The GAM-87A "Skybolt" was to be pylon-launched from B-52s to give it a long-range standoff capability. (USAF/AAHS)

Loaded on to a B-52H, the air-launched Douglas GAM-87A "Skybolt" missile was intended to enter service with SAC, and also be used by the RAF's Vulcan bombers, but was cancelled in December 1962. (USAF)

Left: Air-to-air overhead view of a B-52H in "European one" paint scheme shows its remarkable size and shape. (USAF/ TSgt Bill Thompson)

Below: New engines for the B-52 fleet have been long sought by SAC. In 1969 two B-52Es flew as engine test beds for the General Electric TF-39 turbofans used on the C-5A. Each rated at 40,000lb thrust, they produced as much power as four early J57s used on production B-52s. (USAF/AAHS)

The B-58A Hustler

Convair's supersonic B-58 bomber first flew in November 1956; it carried a crew of three and was equipped with an advanced navigation and bomb-aiming system. It entered service in March 1960, operated by SAC's 43rd and 305th Bombardment Wings. Production was very limited, with 30 development aircraft and 86 production B-58As, with most of the development airframes later converted to training aircraft.

The B-58A had several unique design features. Its three crew members had individual escape capsules in case of ejection at supersonic speeds. The B-58 made extensive use of aluminum honeycomb panels in the airframe and wing, which helped keep the aircraft's structure very light. It was

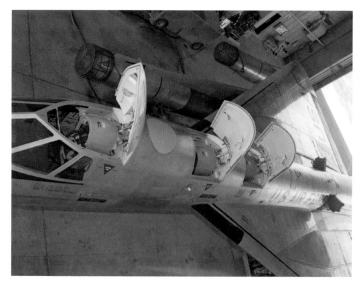

Above left: View showing the B-58As unusual cockpit arrangement for its three crew. (Lockheed Martin)

Above right: The B-58s Stanley escape pod was unique, designed to provide a safe high-speed ejection, protecting the crew member by encasing protective "doors" over them. (NMUSAF)

Right: The test firing of the B-58s Stanley escape pod, with stabilizing fins deployed. (USAF)

the world's first supersonic strategic bomber, capable of Mach 2.2 at altitude and was near supersonic at low level. However, SAC's switch from high-level to low-level operations imposed considerable extra airframe fatigue forces. For anything but the shortest flights, the B-58 needed its huge distinctive under-fuselage fuel tank and required aerial refueling. It initially carried a single nuclear weapon, which had to be positioned under the fuselage in combination with a reshaped external fuel tank. Four external hardpoints were later added, enabling it to carry four smaller B43 or B61 nuclear weapons.

Left: The B-58's supersonic capability made it a very thirsty aircraft and aerial refueling an essential requirement for its SIOP missions. (USAF)

Below: A Convair B-58A fitted with its huge fuel tank. The crane is supporting a large Mk 53 nuclear weapon. This was fitted closest to the aircraft with a reshaped jettisonable fuel tank beneath it. (USAF)

Bottom: B-58A displaying its war load of a fuel tank, Mk 53 and four Mk 43 nuclear bombs. (USAF)

The Hustler's advanced Sperry AN/ASQ-42 bombing and navigation system used a combination of Doppler, stellar, and inertial navigation systems. These married an AN/APN-113 Doppler radar, KS-39 star tracker, search radar, and radar altimeter to provide a highly accurate navigation system. Even with this advanced equipment, the B-58 was a difficult aircraft to master. Accident levels were high, with 26 aircraft lost, and its complex, high-maintenance requirements caused numerous problems in squadron service.

The extraordinarily high cost of the B-58 was another factor held against it, which prevented further development. It had a short service life, with retirements beginning in November 1969 and completed in 1970. The airframes were stored at Davis-Monthan AFB, where 82 of them remained until they were scrapped in 1977.

Above and Below: On December 8, 1964, a taxiing B-58 at Bunker Hill (Grissom) AFB was blown off an icy runway from the jet blast of another B-58 ahead of it. Its main undercarriage leg broke and a fuel tank ruptured and ignited. On board was one Mk 53 and four Mk 43 nuclear weapons. Two of the crew escaped and a third was killed in his ejection capsule. Two weapons remained intact and another scorched, dragged clear by fire crews to a nearby ditch. The final weapon was destroyed by the fire and completely melted. The starboard engines were about the only recognizable parts of the burned aircraft that remained. None of the weapons detonated and the radioactively contaminated wreckage was later buried on base. (C Trott)

The B-58A's defensive armament was a single 20mm-radar-aimed T-171E-3 rotary cannon with 1,200 rounds of ammunition. (NMUSAF/Ty Greenlees)

In the air, Convair's B-58 Hustler looked futuristic, but it was expensive, difficult to fly, and complex to maintain. (USAF)

Chapter 5

Life in SAC

From 1958 one-third of SAC aircraft were placed on fully armed continuous ground alert, with crews at 15-minute readiness for up to a week at a time. For seven years from July 1961, there were also 24-hour airborne alert operations with codenames such as "Chrome Dome," "Hard Hat," and "Giant Lance." These involved the bombers flying specified routes and circling at holding points (such as around Thule AB in Greenland) ready to immediately head toward their targets when ordered. Maintaining the airborne alert posture absorbed vast resources in terms of aerial tankers, fuel usage, crews, support bases, and maintenance personnel. It was also a high-risk activity and given the vast number of hours flown with fully armed aircraft, there were bound to be accidents and these eventually brought an end to the mission in 1968.

Later, commander of SAC's Eighth Air Force, General Buck Shuler, then a B-52 pilot, explained: "The aircraft held up very well; they were fairly new at that time. However, it was fatiguing for the crews – especially on the 25-hour missions." He described: "There was no way we could sleep on the airplanes, but we placed an air mattress in the B-52's lower crew compartment, with the navigators and electronic warfare officers. They could take turns to lie down and rest. Similarly, on the upper deck, we had another air mattress, so the pilots could alternate. On my crew, we ran four-hour cycles. One pilot would be out of his seat and resting. One of the two navigators would do the same. The EWO and the tail gunner could swap out doing the same thing. Generally the co-pilot ran the radios, but when he was resting, either the EWO or the tail gunner took over the responsibility for the UHF and high-frequency radios. On those, we maintained a permanent listening watch with our airborne command post and SAC Headquarters at Offutt AFB in Nebraska."

Gen Shuler later joined the 96th Bomb Wing at Dyess AFB, Texas, from September 1963 to June 1966, flying the "E" model. He described how "one of our alert routes from Dyess ran out to Cape Cod, where we refueled, then flew between the Canada–Greenland gap, over Thule Air Base (AB) out to within 60–90 miles of the North Pole. We then turned left, to come back over Point Barrow in Alaska and air refueled again to fly out almost to the end of the Aleutian Island chain before turning back to make landfall close to the Washington and Oregon state line and returned to Dyess."

The B-52D rear gunner's position. The reclined seat enabled the tail gunner to crawl into position. (USAF/Msgt L Emmett Lewis)

Inside the wing command post, SSgt Don Ave, 2nd BW weapons systems controller keeps track of operations at Barksdale AFB. (USAF/SSgt Phil Schmitten)

Gen Shuler continued, "In addition to flying, we also pulled ground alert. We stayed within the alert facility, with the aircraft cocked and ready to go. In the 9th Bomb Squadron, we had 16 aircraft, with half on ground alert at any given time… We would get regular tests. The klaxon would go and we ran to the aircraft." The exercises were coded: *Alpha*, *Bravo*, *Coco* and *Delta*. The first two involved crews racing to their aircraft and starting engines. "Sometimes it would be a 'Coco' when we taxied the aircraft out to the runway." *Delta* would involve getting airborne and then the alert was cancelled. "All the aircraft could be airborne within 15 minutes. We achieved that by very close, Minimum Interval Take-Offs (MITOs), with just a 15-second gap between departing aircraft."

The "Christmas tree" alert facility for ground alert B-52s at Ellsworth AFB, South Dakota. (USAF/TSgt Boyd Belcher)

SAC's very demanding alert posture was backed by constant testing and evaluation. Most demanding of all were the no-notice Operational Readiness Inspections (ORIs) conducted by the SAC Inspector General (IG). Gen Shuler explained: "When the IG arrived, we would download the weapons from the alert aircraft and generate all 16 bombers for an eight- to ten-hour simulated combat mission ending with recovery back to base."

A B-52 crew jump into an alert vehicle, part of a practice launch exercise during *Global Shield '84*. (USAF/TSgt Boyd Belcher)

B-52s sitting on a misty alert flightline at Grand Forks AFB, North Dakota in 1981. (USAF/ MSgt Bob Wickley)

Smoke trails from three B-52Gs launching on a minimum interval take-off exercise as part of an 18 aircraft departure under combat conditions. (USAF/SSgt Phil Schmitten)

On the IGs order, "we would launch with a MITO and often follow it with a navigation leg, sometimes at night. Then we would hit a tanker, to demonstrate our air-refueling proficiency. A "Sprite profile," could follow. This was a low-level leg flown between 500ft and 1,000ft, ending with a radar bomb-scoring run against a range where, using electronic tones, they scored our bombing accuracy. We might then fly another navigation leg back to base." Once on the ground, crews would then often be required to "take a battery of written tests to ensure we understood the tactical doctrine and what was required of us. We were constantly being tested – obviously very important when you were dealing with nuclear weapons."

Restricted to their alert facilities or air bases for long periods at a time, alert drills and snap inspections would keep alert crews busy, but individuals often had to deal with extensive periods of inactivity. Learning checklists, operational procedures, and related tasks were important, but crews often found hobbies, studied for promotions, or followed higher education courses to fill their time.

"Bent Spears" and "Broken Arrows"

Holding nuclear bombers and missiles on armed alert inevitably posed possibilities for catastrophic accidents. Many early incidents were kept "hidden" within the SAC and Department of Defense communities, but some were just too big or public to conceal. "Bent Spear" was the codeword adopted to describe a wide range of situations involving warhead accidents when there was not a serious risk of them leaking radiation or being seized by hostile actors. Much more serious were the "Broken Arrows." These covered a wide range of incidents generally described as being an actual accident involving a nuclear weapon, warhead, or any of its major components. This can include unauthorized launch, a nuclear detonation, or the jettisoning of a nuclear weapon. There were around 30 Broken Arrows

SAC B-47s were forward deployed to Sidi Slimane AB in French Morocco. On January 31, 1958, A taxiing B-47's wheels caught fire, engulfing the aircraft, which burned out and melted its nuclear weapon into the taxiway. (USAF)

during the Cold War, but the accuracy of that figure is difficult to assess because of the secrecy that still surrounds some of them. The rate of incidents slowed over the years due to several factors, including reductions in the stockpile, improved safety features on the weapons, more stringent handling and storage procedures, and probably most important of all, changes to weapon movement procedures, ground alerts, and the ending of airborne alert missions.

Major accidents have happened to all the aircraft types operated by SAC, from the B-29 through to the B-50 – the jettisoning of weapons from B-36s and numerous incidents involving B-47s including the conflagration and "melting" of a B-47 and its weapon on an airfield taxiway in Morocco. Several B-52s, the most reliable of SAC's bombers, have experienced serious accidents too, particularly during the period of airborne alert operations. Near Goldsboro, North Carolina, in the early hours of January 24, 1961, a KC-135A crew noticed their B-52 receiver leaking fuel. As the B-52 attempted to recover into Seymour Johnson AFB, it broke-up, with the two Mk 39 nuclear bombs it was carrying falling to Earth. A portion of one bomb's nuclear core has never been recovered, buried so deeply in the ground that it prevented recovery. Revealed in recent years is the belief that one of its bombs came close to detonation when the mechanical links designed to prevent accidental detonation failed. Three crew perished in the accident.

On January 17, 1966, a KC-135A and B-52G on a *Chrome Dome* mission collided close to the Spanish Mediterranean fishing port of Palomares. The four tanker-crew members and three of the B-52 crew were killed and debris was spread over a wide area. All the weapons were eventually recovered, one later from the sea, but there was significant radioactive contamination of local farmland. This incident, and another at Thule AB in Greenland on January 21, 1968, hastened the end of continuous airborne alert. A crew-compartment fire caused the crew to abandon their B-52; one man died and the aircraft crashed on to sea ice close to the base. The high-explosive components of its four nuclear weapons detonated, spreading contamination. The ensuing review and political row saw airborne alert operations suspended.

SAC's missile force suffered major accidents too. The most serious loss of life was when a Titan II exploded in a silo at a launch center in Arkansas in August 1965, killing 53 construction workers. Another explosion occurred in September 1980 at a launch silo close to Damascus in Arkansas. A spanner was dropped inside a silo, rupturing a Titan II's liquid fuel tank. Some hours later it exploded, devastating the underground launch complex.

Above: The collision between a KC-135A and B-52G on a *Chrome Dome* flight on January 17, 1966, near Palomares, Spain, killed four tanker crew members and three from the B-52. Its four Mk 28 weapons were all eventually recovered but there was significant local contamination. (Kit Talbot)

Left: The final B28 nuclear bomb from the Palomares "Broken Arrow" was recovered by a Spanish fishing boat during a massive search, four months after the accident. (Sandia Labs)

The result of the explosion of a Titan missile in its silo at Damascus, Arkansas, in 1980. It blew apart the two hinged 115-ton concrete and steel doors that covered the missile. (Greg Devlin)

Chapter 6

Missile Forces

S AC's missile forces became a key element of its nuclear triad as the force and related technology matured during the 1960s. Serious research began after the end of World War Two, and the early stages were aided by German rocket scientists spirited to the US. America was already developing numerous nuclear missile designs when the USSR launched Sputnik 1 on October 4, 1957, which generated political and public panic about Soviet missile capabilities.

Early missile types experienced considerable difficulties. Initially, their lack of power meant they could only carry small warheads and with poor levels of accuracy they were only useful for striking large "soft" targets such as cities. The mechanical reliability of the weapons was often doubtful, with test failures leading to many spectacular explosions on launch pads and in flight. The ill-fated Northrop SM-62 Snark was a good example of the difficulties that affected several early programs; a cruise missile with wings, it emerged from large numbers of proposed designs in the early post-war years. With flight tests in 1951–52, development of its propulsion and navigation systems proved tortuous and the weapon's costs spiraled. During 1951 severe criticisms of its complexity and poor performance grew. Intended to become operational in 1953, Snark's constant failure to meet accuracy requirements, with misses averaging five miles from the intended target, meant a more powerful warhead was necessary. Snark remained notoriously unreliable; deliveries began in January 1958 and led to its withdrawal in June 1961.

The ICBM Missile Gallery at the National Museum of the US Air Force, Dayton, Ohio. (NMUSAF)

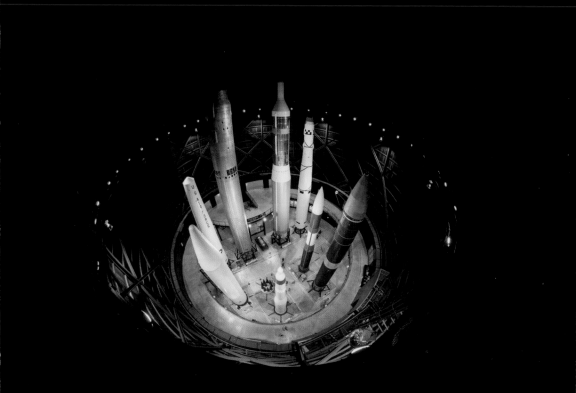

Northrop's SM-62 Snark was so notoriously unreliable that it was withdrawn by SAC in 1961, less then three years after it entered service. (USAF)

The US Navy was developing its own Lockheed Polaris submarine-launched missile, while the US Army backed Chrysler's Jupiter medium-range missile (taken over by the air force) and deployed to Italy and Turkey. The USAF was managing competing programs from Douglas for the Thor (later stationed in eastern England), General Dynamic's Atlas, Martin's Titan, and Boeing's Minuteman. The nuclear hysteria of the time did not concentrate on a single missile system but instead pushed all into production. In service, this caused considerable duplication, as each type required highly specialized equipment, training, and handling. All were very high-cost programs and their respective development paths were often difficult, with many failures before a reasonable degree of reliability was eventually achieved.

Above left: A Douglas SM-75 PGM-17A Thor missile being erected ready for launch. (NMUSAF)

Above right: Missiles, like this Thor, were frequently moved, without warheads by USAF C-133 aircraft. (NMUSAF)

SAC Jupiter medium-range missiles were based in Turkey and Italy. When sat upright above ground, they were extremely vulnerable to conventional or nuclear attack. (USAF)

Having around a 1,500-mile (2,400km) range, the Thor and Jupiter missiles were classed as Intermediate-range Ballistic Missiles (ICBMs). They had to be based relatively close to the enemy, hence their deployment to Italy, Turkey, and the UK. Both types used highly volatile liquid fuels and sat in the open. They had to be erected from their horizontal storage positions before they could be fueled and fired from specially built launch pads. The time taken to do this, their forward location, and open positions made them extremely vulnerable and tempting targets for a pre-emptive Soviet strike. Thor missiles were first deployed in 1958, with Jupiter in Italy and Turkey in 1961. Both types were withdrawn from Europe in 1963.

Time sequence showing an Atlas E being erected, fueled and launched from its semi-hardened "coffin" pen. (USAF)

Vandenberg AFB, on the Californian coast, was transferred to the USAF in late 1956. Its position was ideal for test launches, aiming for missile ranges established far across the Pacific at Eniwetok and Kwajalein, in the US Marshall Islands. Vandenberg became the location where test launch facilities were constructed for all the US ballistic missile types developed. Although primarily a test establishment, it also served briefly as an operational base. From April 1, 1956, it became home to SAC's 576th Strategic Missile Squadron, the command's first ICBM unit equipped with Atlas missiles. It took over its first alert on October 31, 1959, and the site remained operational until the squadron was stood down on April 2, 1966. Ever since, Vandenberg has continued as a missile test and space launch facility.

The Convair/General Dynamics Atlas missile was the first true intercontinental missile to enter SAC service, but it was an interim weapon. Three versions of this liquid-fueled missile were in operational service between October 1959 and April 1965. The Atlas D had a range of around 9,000 miles (14,500km) and stationed at FE Warren AFB in Wyoming and Offutt AFB in Nebraska. They were stored upright above ground and fueled just prior to launch, but with just minimal protection, they were also extremely vulnerable. The Atlas E was deployed to FE Warren AFB, Forbes AFB in Kansas, and Fairchild AFB, Washington. These were stored lying down in semi-hardened "coffins" with the missile raised to the vertical for firing. The Atlas F was the most widely used, deployed to Schilling in Kansas; Lincoln AFB, Nebraska; Altus AFB in Oklahoma; Dyess AFB in Texas; Walker AFB, New

Launched from Vandenberg AFB, six dummy Minuteman III Mk 12 MIRVs approach targets at the Kwajalein Atoll range during a test on July 10, 1979. (USAF)

Mexico; and Plattsburgh AFB, New York. The Atlas F was kept stored vertically in silos and in an alert would have been fueled and raised to the surface by a lift and fired. It could be launched in roughly ten minutes, which shaved about five minutes off the Atlas D and E launch process. Around 350 Atlases of all versions were built and deployment peaked at 79 missiles in 1963. All were withdrawn by April 1965 as early Titan and Minuteman weapons became operational, with many Atlas's later re-purposed for space launches.

Mighty Titan

The Titan I was built as a fallback design, in case the development of the Atlas failed, but was itself nearly cancelled on several occasions during successive rounds of budget cuts. Some 62 flight tests took place between 1959 and 1962. Titan I took 15 minutes to fuel up and be carried to the surface by an elevator and launched above ground. The 101 missiles built meant that, at any one time, 54 were deployed to the six operational strategic missile squadrons – two at Lowry AFB, Colorado; one each at Beale AFB, at Ellsworth in South Dakota, and Larson AFB, Washington; and another to Mountain Home AFB in Idaho. The Titan I had a 7,000-mile (11,250km) range but was only in service between 1961 and 1965, being withdrawn as the Minuteman and Titan II became available.

Time lapse of a Titan 1 test from Vandenberg AFB. On receipt of a launch order, the missile was fueled below ground, which took around 15 minutes. It was then lifted above ground by an elevator before blasting off toward its target. (USAF)

A SAC Titan II missile test launch from Vandenberg AB in 1978. The missile was capable of carrying a 9-megaton warhead. (USAF)

Titan II entered service in 1962 and was a major advance for ICBM operations. Its rocket motors were powered by newly developed, less volatile, and corrosive fuels that could remain in the Titan's II's fuel tanks for long periods without the need to either launch or be de-fueled. They could now be launched within one minute from vertical silos buried deep below ground, making them almost invulnerable to Soviet attack. The Titan II was a two-stage rocket, again viewed as an interim platform, likely to be in service for a maximum of five to seven years. Three wings, operating 54 missiles between them, with the 308th Strategic Missile Wing (SMW) at Little Rock AFB in Kansas, the 381st SMW at McConnell AFB in Wichita, and the 390th SMW at Davis-Monthan in Arizona; each wing comprised two squadrons. The 10,000 miles (16,100km) of Titan II's range was highly valued as it could carry a huge 9-megaton payload, ideal for striking deeply buried Soviet command and control facilities. In 1967 the Titan II fleet peaked at 63 missiles and its retirement was rescheduled for 1971. However, once the internal guidance and other systems were updated, the gradual phase-out didn't begin until July 1982. Two serious accidents in 1978 and 1980 hastened the demise as ageing fuel seal issues and increasing maintenance requirements began to take their toll. The last operational Titan II unit was the 381st SMW at Little Rock, Arkansas, its last nine missiles only retired in 1987.

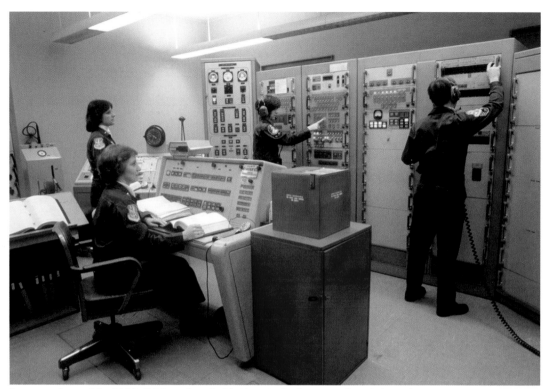

Crew members of the 308th SMW, equipped with Titan II missiles, at work at Little Rock AFB in March 1983. (USAF)

Minuteman

The LGM-30 Minuteman I missile brought maturity to SAC's missile force. Produced in three major versions, it became the mainstay of the SAC's missile force, has been regularly updated, and remains in service today. Its solid fuel meant it too could withstand long periods of duty, ready to launch without the same level of maintenance support required for the Atlas and Titan. Development work began in the 1950s and in December 1962 the first two flights of ten missiles became operational with squadrons of the 341st SMW at Malmstrom AFB, Montana. Targeting systems and warhead accuracy were soon enhanced and the improved Minuteman III was introduced to service with the 91st SMW at Minot AFB, North Dakota, in 1970. This new version meant each missile carried three smaller warheads – Multiple Independently targetable Re-entry Vehicles (MIRVs) or decoys. The Minuteman III, with many subsequent upgrades, remains at the forefront of the US nuclear deterrent.

A 321st SMW crew member works at his control panel inside a Minuteman III Launch Control Center in 1983. (USAF/SSgt Louis Comeger)

Little is visible above ground of the Minuteman III Launch Facility Site "Sierra 34" near Malmstrom AFB, Montana, in July 1979. (USAF)

SAC used UH-1Hs to move technicians to many of its remote missile silo locations, such as this one at Badlands Loop, South Dakota. (Mark Wilderman, National Parks Service)

Above: "Somewhere in Wyoming," a USAF UH-1 flies close to a Missile Alert Facility, carrying troops prepared to defend the remote nuclear silo. (USAF/SSgt Scott Wagers)

Right: In the foreground a Minuteman missile from Launch Facility 08 (LF-08) at Vandenberg AFB just clears its silo. Another Minuteman missile launched some seconds earlier from LF-09 is already well into its launch. (USAF/ MSgt Arvan Washington)

Chapter 7

Crisis and War

The early 1960s saw a remarkable convergence of developments that significantly changed the shape of SAC. During the Eisenhower administration, a congressional frenzy of defense spending, fueled by pressures from the major aerospace companies, saw the development of a plethora of aircraft and missile types that soon entered service. However, most lacked the range and power that SAC required. Thanks to CIA U-2 overflights of the USSR from 1956, President Eisenhower and senior commanders already knew that the highly politicized Soviet bomber and missile gaps were far from reality. Khrushchev's bluster that the USSR was producing thousands of missiles able to hit the continental USA was just a bluff. At best the USSR possessed large numbers of intermediate-range missiles, able to destroy western Europe but not the mainland United States.

President Kennedy assumed office in January 1961 and together with his Secretary of Defense, Robert McNamara, faced several serious issues with major implications for SAC. The Goldsboro B-52 crash and near nuclear disaster on January 23, 1961, had occurred just days after McNamara assumed office. This raised serious weapons safety issues and he soon received the Weapons Systems Evaluation Group (WSEG) Report No. 50. This detailed the approximately nine times higher cost of keeping a B-52 on ground alert compared to the Navy's Polaris and Minuteman missiles entering service. It also

identified the woeful state of US nuclear command and control arrangements and the vulnerability of SAC's critical communications. It further highlighted the inadequacy of early warning systems and the "continuity of government" arrangements in the face of a surprise attack. In response, to reduce the possible effects of a surprise attack, a larger proportion of SAC's air fleet was placed on ground alert, so that by June 1960 more than 450 bombers and 230 tankers were at their bases ready to launch. Perhaps even more serious was the state of the SIOP. It was essentially a one-strike plan, requiring only a "go code" that would launch the whole attack plan without nuance to adjust in less catastrophic situations. Even more vulnerable were the many US nuclear weapons stationed in Europe.

The improvements identified during this period took years to produce results but eventually had a profound effect on SAC operations. These included

A maintenance standardization and evaluation team inspector observes as a 93rd BW team loads B-61 nuclear bombs on to a B-52 during SAC's 1985 Combat Weapons Loading Competition. (USAF/SSgt Bob Simons)

Closest to the camera are AGM-69 short-range attack missiles and Mk 28 nuclear weapons in the bomb bay of a B-52H during Exercise *Global Shield 1984*. (USAF/TSgt Boyd Belcher)

the evolution of a more nuanced SIOP, better weapon safety devices installed to prevent accidental or unauthorized detonation, improved command and control arrangements, more survivable communications, and the creation of airborne backup command, control, and alternate launch mechanisms. Perhaps most profound of all was the recognition that SACs bombers had had their day. Now, high-level operations were nearly impossible due to vast improvements in Soviet air defense missiles. The bombers only real chance of penetration was extremely low-level flying, which increased airframe fatigue to aircraft originally designed for high-altitude operations. It also required new crew training and tactics, placing even more demands on them. McNamara decreed that no new bombers be developed; the prototype XB-70 Valkyrie was abandoned and much greater reliance was placed on SAC and US Navy missile forces.

Cuban Missile Crisis

While there had been a bubbling crisis in Berlin during 1960–61, that which started in Cuba during 1962 almost had cataclysmic consequences. The discovery of Khrushchev's plan to install medium-range missiles in western Cuba, during the autumn of 1962, brought a sudden shock to the US strategic environment. Immediately the southern continental US was very vulnerable to Soviet nuclear attack, and the standoff that quickly unfolded was the closest SAC and the US ever came to nuclear war. Joint Chiefs' plans to undertake air strikes on the island were not sanctioned and instead a blockade was imposed on Cuba. US forces went to Defense Condition 2 (DEFCON 2) for the first time ever. Polaris submarines left their ports, SAC dispersed its bomber force, and some 200 B-47s were spread between large numbers of civilian airfields, with some crews sleeping by their aircraft. The number of B-52s on airborne alert was increased to around 65 aircraft and all others were placed on ground alert.

Pressure on Kennedy to engage in airstrikes against Cuba peaked on October 27, 1963, when SAC's Major Rudolph Anderson, flying a U-2 borrowed from the CIA, was shot down over Cuba and killed. Fortunately, after secret negotiations, on October 28, Khrushchev announced the Soviet's decision to withdraw its missiles from Cuba and the crisis gradually defused.

General Shuler was a 7th Bomb Wing (BW) B-52 co-pilot during the Cuba crisis. He explained: "All training missions were cancelled and every B-52 and B-47 was loaded with nuclear weapons. The B-47s were deployed to forward locations. Each bomb wing was flying two continuous airborne alert aircraft. We were cocked and ready to go. I remember President Kennedy coming on the TV while I was on ground alert. Things looked pretty grim. We had an alert changeover, so I quickly went home to get clean flying suits and clothes and immediately went back to continue the ground alert. It was a very tense period. I didn't go home for 30 days, nobody did. I figured it was a 50/50 chance that we might have a nuclear war."

The 7th BW's aircraft maintained dedicated patrol routes as he described. During the crisis, after the bombers took off, "we would coast out, close to Savannah, Georgia, and maintained a passing watch over the Soviet ships in the area… We flew from Carswell AFB over to the northwest corner of Spain and refueled with a KC-135 tanker. Close to the Balearic Islands we would turn back and rendezvous with another KC-135 near Gibraltar. This filled the B-52s fuel tanks for our return trip back across the Atlantic." During this period of heightened airborne alert, SAC launched more than 2,000 sorties and accumulated nearly 50,000 flight hours without a major accident.

South East Asia

As the US became ever more deeply embroiled in South East Asia, SAC became involved in its second shooting war, as its B-52s forward deployed to Andersen AFB on Guam. However, the mission was not one that SAC was fully prepared for. The command realized it would have to reconfigure its B-52s, the only aircraft with sufficient range and a large bombload suitable for the task. Dedicated to the nuclear mission, conventional bombing operations were not something SAC had seriously trained for. In November 1964 the Joint Chiefs of Staff (JCS) recommended to Robert McNamara that the USAF commence strategic bombing operations against North Vietnam. However, fears that using B-52s might widen the conflict delayed the decision to commit them.

B-52Ds from the 7th BW and 320th BW flew their first *Arc Light* mission on June 18, 1965, against North Vietnam. They dropped 1,000lb and 750lb iron bombs on unseen Viet Cong jungle positions from high level, losing two 7th BW B-52s in a collision. To increase their "iron bomb" capacity, 80 B-52Ds received a "Big Belly" modification. This enabled 84 500lb bombs to be squeezed into their internal bomb bay, with another 24 mounted externally on two wing pylons. Soon the B-52 raids were averaging 8,000 tons of bombs a month. In 1967 the U Tapao AB in Thailand also became available to the B-52s. This meant missions could be completed in under four hours, rather than the 16 to 18 hours and aerial refueling required for Guam-based operations. To provide sufficient crews, B-52 training at Castle AFB was rapidly expanded, as were bomb supplies to sustain the pace of operations. Crews from G and H models went on fortnight-long courses to qualify them to fly the older D models in South East Asia. All of this was achieved while SAC maintained its SIOP commitment.

By 1968 the B-52s in South East Asia were flying an average of 1,800 sorties a month, but by June 1972, sortie numbers had reached 3,150. The climax of B-52 operations in South East Asia came with the *Linebacker* missions in 1972. Mission planning involved three nights of heavy bombing, with waves attacking Hanoi and Haiphong, supported by other aircraft. The initial attack comprised 42 B-52Ds from U Tapao, 54 B-52Gs, and 33 B-52Ds from Andersen, with 93 sorties planned for the second night and 99 for the third.

The B-52F had a maximum 10,000lb internal bombload for operations over South East Asia. Twenty-eight B-52Fs were fitted with external racks for 24 of the 750lb bombs in June 1964, later followed by an additional 46 aircraft. (USAF)

The manufacture of special removable bomb racks fitted to B-52Ds enabled them to carry much larger conventional bombloads over other versions of the Stratofortress. (USAF)

Guam held around 155 bombers spread over five miles of parking ramps, making the mass bomber launches extremely complex. On the evening of December 18, 1972, they departed in loose cells of three, intended to give maximum mutual Electronic CounterMeasures (ECM) cover. As they approached their targets USAF EB-66 Destroyers, US Navy EA-3 Skywarriors, and EA-6 Prowlers were already at work jamming North Vietnamese radar and radio frequencies. Two-seat F-105F/Gs provided "Wild Weasel" Surface-to-Air Missile (SAM) suppression support, while more air force and navy aircraft hit Vietnamese airfields to keep enemy fighters on the ground. More F-4s provided Combat Air Patrol (CAP) and escort for any damaged aircraft. On the first night, over 200 SAMs were fired at the B-52s – with two aircraft from Guam and one from U Tapao being lost. On the second night's mission, no aircraft were lost, but the third saw two B-52Ds and four B-52Gs shot down. Three more successive days of attacks saw no further losses, but a day's respite on December 25 saw the North Vietnamese rush to replenish and restore their SAM sites. The following night saw the most dramatic attacks: 33 B-52Ds and 45 B-52Gs left their airfields within two and a half hours, four waves striking at Hanoi from different directions. Three more waves hit targets in Haiphong. All the attacks were co-ordinated to take place at the same time, supported by another 110 other aircraft. Two B-52s were lost. Over the next four nights, more attacks struck at individual SAM sites and then the missile storage depots again. Two more B-52s were lost before the operation ended. In *Linebacker II*'s 11 days, SAC had mounted 729 sorties, dropped 15,000 tons of bombs, and lost 15 aircraft and their valuable crews. Around 1,240 SAMs were fired at them.

In total, US operations dropped a greater tonnage of bombs on South East Asia than were used on Germany and Japan combined, during World War Two. The statistics for B-52 operations alone from 1965 to 1973 are staggering. More than 126,600 sorties were flown against targets in South Vietnam, North Vietnam, Laos, and Cambodia, with 26 B-52s lost to enemy action and accidents. The end of the wars in South East Asia eased the enormous pressures on SAC and meant it could return to concentrate on its nuclear mission.

B-52s stretch to the horizon at Andersen AFB, Guam, during preparations for *Linebacker* missions in 1972. (USAF)

Above: A B-52D parked at its dispersal in South East Asia in 1975. (AAHS/ NARA)

Right: B-52D at Andersen AFB. Unmodified B-52Ds could carry 27 x 500lb or 750lb, but the "Big Belly" modified aircraft could carry up to 84 x 500lb or 42 x 750lb. (NMUSAF)

Chapter 8

New Aircraft and Missiles

General Dynamics FB-111A

Selected in 1965 to replace the B-58 and early B-52 variants, the FB-111A was regarded as a stopgap medium bomber by SAC. The initial plan for around 263 airframes was heavily cut in 1969 to just 76, with deliveries between 1969 and 1971. These were allocated to the 380th Bombardment Wing (Medium) at Plattsburgh AFB, New York and the 509th BW (Medium) at Pease AFB, New Hampshire. The FB-111A had an improved navigation fit over previous F-111 variants, which included a star tracker, an automated weapons release system, and a satellite communications receiver. Weaponry could include two internal and up to four external pylon-mounted AGM-69 SRAM missiles or free-fall nuclear weapons; the external weaponry could be switched for extra fuel tanks. There were plans to modify the FB-111As into a much-improved FB-111H variant, but these were dropped when the B-1B program was re-invigorated under President Reagan. As the B-1Bs were delivered, SAC's FB-111As were gradually withdrawn, the first leaving the 509th BW in June 1990, the remaining aircraft being dropped from the SAC inventory during 1991.

Above: An FB-111A taking off from Pease AFB, New Hampshire, in 1984. (Sgt Robert F Young)

Left: A 509th Bomb Wing FB-111A and its ordnance load. On the wing pylons are 20 BDU-50 500lb practice bombs. In the front row (L to R): an M-117D 750lb high-drag bomb, 12 Mk 106 5lb practice bombs and a Mk 82 500lb high-drag bomb. Behind them are practice B-83 and B-61 nuclear bombs and two AGM-69A SRAM missiles. (USAF/MSgt Ken Hammond)

Above: Superlative low-level performer, two 509th BW FB-111As carrying Mk 82 practice bombs. (USAF/MSgt Ken Hammond)

Right: A 715th BS FB-111A is refueled by a 509th ARS KC-135A during exercise *Proud Shield '87*. (USAF)

The KC-10A

As US airlift and tanker resources became increasingly overstretched during the 1970s, the USAF sought an advanced tanker cargo aircraft. McDonnell Douglas's KC-10A "Extender" won an initial 12-aircraft contract on December 19, 1977, with a first flight on July 12, 1980. In total, SAC acquired 60 KC-10As and assigned them equally between three wings. The first KC-10As were delivered to the 2nd BW's, 32nd Air Refueling Squadron (ARS) at Barksdale AFB, Louisiana, and they soon joined the 22nd Air Refueling Wing (ARW) at March AFB, California, and finally the 68th ARW at Seymour Johnson AFB, North Carolina. Even today the KC-10A's performance remains impressive, able to carry mixed payloads of fuel, cargo, and passengers.

In 1981 Lt Col Jon Mickley was an early KC-10A pilot, already very experienced on KC-135s. He explained, "The KC-10A was unlike any other airplane in the air force. The magic thing about it was we could be air-refueled ourselves. The airplane hauled vast amounts of fuel great distances; could carry up to 75 people and 17 cargo pallets. This gave the KC-10A a unique capability and it fulfilled this dual role better than anything else in the world."

Retired Col Victor Herrera, another 4,000-hour veteran KC-10A pilot and former squadron commander, explained why the KC-10A was never fully integrated into the SIOP: "KC-135s would be loaded with fuel and sit on the ramp until ordered to launch. When they did this with the KC-10As, they started leaking. Modified from the commercial DC-10 airliner, where you just loaded the fuel required and went straightaway, its fuel bladders were not designed to just sit full of fuel for long periods. Although the problem was later fixed, the KC-10A had to be treated differently from the KC-135. That was sort of good for us because it meant the KC-10As were never fully committed to SIOP operations, where we sat on constant alert."

During their early years, KC-10As wore this smart white with blue cheatline paint scheme. (USAF/CMSgt D Sutherland)

Right: One great attribute of the KC-10A was its capability to be air-refueled. (USAF)

Below: The spacious interior of the KC-10A meant it could be readily adapted to carry a mix of passengers and freight. (USAF)

Left: The KC-10A's boom operator position was far more comfortable than their counterparts on KC-135s, who had to lie prone in their working position. (USAF/SSgt Schading)

Below: The KC-10As flexibility made it far better suited to daily operations than sitting on ground SIOP alert. (USAF)

Rockwell B-1 Lancer

Despite its comparative youth when compared to the B-52, the B-1 was perhaps SAC's most undervalued aircraft. The B-1 was designed as a high-speed, low-level, deep penetration bomber, with the first prototype flying in December 1974. In June 1977, facing rapidly escalating costs President Jimmy Carter cancelled B-1 procurement but permitted further development and testing. When Ronald Reagan became US president in January 1981, defense funding moved into the fast lane, and in January 1982 Rockwell was contracted to develop the B-1B. The first "new" design flew in October 1984. Rapidly pushed into service, it joined the 96th BW in 1986 and by 1988, all 100 were delivered to equip squadrons of the 28th, 319th, and 384th Bomb Wings in the nuclear role, with later modifications for conventional operations.

Above: When Ronald Reagan became President, development of the B-1B was rapidly accelerated. (SSgt USAF Bill Thompson)

Right: The first production B-1B towed out of Rockwell's production facility in September 1984. (USAF/MSgt Mike Dial)

A B-1B banks during an acceptance flight conducted in 1987. (USAF)

Peacekeeper

After a protracted development, the first of 50 LGM-118A Peacekeeper missiles entered service in late 1986, with the 90th SMW at FE Warren AFB. The ability of each missile to carry 12 independent warheads or decoys made it a potent system. However, the reductions in US–Soviet tensions during the mid-1980s put a brake on further major developments and production. Peacekeepers remained operational until the withdrawal of the final missiles in 2005.

An LGM-118A Peacekeeper missile is test fired from Vandenberg AFB in February 1989. (USAF/CMSgt Don Sutherland)

European Cold War Missions

After heavy operations in Vietnam, SAC's older B-52Ds were showing serious signs of fatigue. In 1972 a modification program began, which included rebuilding the wings of the "best" 80 remaining airframes.

From the late 1970s, B-52Ds were increasingly deployed for European operations from UK airfields, used as forward operating bases. SAC envisaged that conventional missions would mostly be conducted by round-trip flights, originating from their US bases. However, such flights absorbed huge amounts of aerial refueling resources; the tankers were already required for other vital missions in the run-up to general war and so made forward basing attractive. Wartime tasks envisaged for any European-based SAC B-52Ds included show of force, area denial, precision attack, and defense suppression missions, alongside maritime surveillance, minelaying, and reconnaissance missions.

Right: A 1970s view of the Davis Monthan boneyard as many B-52Ds and B-52Fs await disposal. (USAF)

Below: B-52G 80189 from the 379th BW based at Wurtsmith AFB lifts off during a forward basing exercise at RAF Marham in 1980. (Chris Chennell)

Above: The B-52Ds huge ordnance-carrying capability made it a conventional bomber par excellence. (USAF)

Left: A Guam-based deployed B-52D dropping a mine during Exercise *Team Spirit '82*. (USAF)

Below: A B-52G during a low-level aerial mining mission off the South Korean coast during Exercise *Team Spirit '86*. (USAF)

Chapter 9

"SAC Recon"

S AC's task of eliminating Soviet nuclear bomber and missile capabilities made it a huge consumer of target intelligence. As most had to be gained by aerial means, it was not unreasonable that SAC had a significant role in intelligence collection. SAC aircraft used in reconnaissance roles included RB-29s, RB-36s, RB-45s, RB-47s, RB-50s, RC-135s, U-2s, and SR-71s. Many of these missions required SAC to work in conjunction with the USAF Security Service and its European and Pacific commands. SAC aircraft patrolled the periphery of the Soviet bloc almost daily, soaking up radio and electronic transmissions. Up to 1956, SAC also engaged in some major deep penetration operations of the USSR to collect the target imagery it required. After that, it became heavily reliant on CIA U-2 overflights and, from August 1960 onwards, on satellite imagery managed through the National Reconnaissance Office.

The most audacious SAC overflight operation, codenamed *Home Run*, was conducted in 1956. In January, Curtis LeMay, approved the deployment of 16 RB-47Es from the 28th Strategic Reconnaissance Wing and four RB-47Hs from the 55th SRW to Thule AB in Greenland. Arriving there on March 21, 1956, high winds, snow, and temperatures regularly down to minus 37 degrees celsius made conditions challenging. Operations were dependent on the 30 KC-97s that accompanied them to provide air refueling. From Thule, flights followed assigned routes that covered the entire northern coast of the USSR from Novaya Zemlya in the west to the airfields on the Chukchi Peninsula in the east. At least one flight crossed the Soviet coast at Tiksi and penetrated roughly 650 miles inland to image two Soviet airfields. Flown from early April to early May, these totaled an incredible 156 flights, including a "mass mission finale" of six RB-47s on 6–7 May 1956.

91st SRW RB-45Cs were heavily involved in very sensitive early SAC reconnaissance operations. (NMUSAF)

SAC's largest deep penetration reconnaissance operation was probably *Home Run* in 1956, which saw many RB-47E and H missions deep, deep into Soviet airspace. (USAF)

SAC's RB-47H aircraft flew risky peripheral reconnaissance missions around the USSR. Losses included the shooting down of one in July 1960 over international waters in the Barents Sea. Only two of the six crew members survived. (USAF)

SAC briefly operated a small number of RB-57D/Fs in the reconnaissance role, with their best-known mission being on December 11, 1956. Six aircraft from the 4025th SRS took off from Yokota AB in Japan and split into two groups. One group conducted a feint while the other proceeded to fly directly over Vladivostok to image the city, port, and surrounding areas. The size of the operation and the feint alerted all Soviet air defenses in the region. The mission was clearly a significant one to SAC, as LeMay was present at Yokota and awarded medals to the returning participants. The flight provoked a very robust and detailed Soviet protest. Eisenhower immediately prohibited further penetration flights for a while and terminated the USAF's "Sensint" overflight reconnaissance program. At its 1956 peak, SAC operated 574 aircraft dedicated to the reconnaissance role; however, as the CIA U-2 and National Reconnaissance Office (NRO) satellite programs began to yield significant results, that number had dropped to just 32 aircraft in 1965, most of which were engaged in electronic signals collection.

SAC U-2s from the 4080th SRW moved to Laughlin AFB in April 1957 and relocated to Davis-Monthan in July 1963. They were mostly employed in fallout monitoring missions around the world but were more publicly identified with monitoring Soviet build-up in Cuba during 1962. From 1964, SAC U-2s deployed to Thailand to support operations in South East Asia. They became the 100th SRW in late June 1966, moving to Beale AFB in July 1976 to join the 9th SRW and operate alongside its SR-71s there. From Beale AFB, the wing maintained a forward presence at Osan AB in South Korea by 1978. From the mid-1970s SAC U-2Rs returned to Europe with temporary deployments to RAF Mildenhall, their SIGINT equipment used to monitor Soviet and Warsaw Pact communications and movements. From RAF Akrotiri in Cyprus, SAC U-2Rs had taken on tasks inherited from the CIA in 1974, flying SIGINT missions over the eastern Mediterranean. They also inherited photographic overflights of the demarcation lines between Israeli and Egyptian forces in the Sinai and Syrian positions in the Golan Heights, following the 1973 Yom Kippur War.

In October 1982, SAC's 17th Reconnaissance Wing was established at RAF Alconbury to operate its newly built U-2Rs, designated as "TR-1s." While owned by SAC, the TR-1s were largely tasked by United States Air Forces in Europe (USAFE) to fly missions over West Germany, and occasionally elsewhere as required. They collected electronic transmissions from deep into Warsaw Pact and Soviet territory for re-transmission to a ground base at "Metro Tango" in West Germany for analysis.

Serious wing fatigue issues meant the RB-57F had only a short career with SAC. (AAHS/Chuck Stewart Collection)

SAC's 17th RW TR-1As from RAF Alconbury flew SIGINT missions along Warsaw Pact borders during the 1980s. (CMSgt Don Sutherland)

The TR-1s at RAF Alconbury required the construction of extra wide Hardened Aircraft Shelters to protect them. (USAF)

SR-71 Blackbird

In late August 1959, Lockheed won the competition to develop the CIA's exotic Mach 3 plus A-12 "Oxcart," which later became the SR-71 "Blackbird," and first flew on 25 April 1962. SAC's 4020th SRW at Beale AFB became the SR-71s parent unit in 1965, with the first aircraft arriving in January 1966. In June 1966 it became the 9th SRW.

A constant feature of the SR-71 program was its high cost. Maintenance was highly specialist, as were the necessary support facilities. Its thirsty Pratt & Whitney J-58 engines meant SR-71s required frequent air-to-air refueling provided by special KC-135Qs, which carried the SR-71s JP-7 fuel, from the now 100th ARW, co-located at Beale AFB. While the Blackbirds could fly missions direct from the US, forward detachments were established at RAF Mildenhall in the UK and Kadena AB in Japan. The first brief deployments to the UK took place from 1976 until becoming permanent in 1982, primarily monitoring the Barents Sea and Soviet troop rotations.

Still heavily redacted, a formerly "secret" 1982 SAC history describes how the use of the SR-71s optical cameras was problematic in central and northern Europe, given the high prevalence of cloud cover. However, the use of High Resolution Radar (HRR) sensors was much less affected by cloud and as the technology matured it produced ever better quality imagery. The US Navy was particularly keen on HRR missions because its cloud-penetrating capabilities enabled regular imaging of Soviet naval activity around the Kola Peninsula and Barents Sea areas. These areas were home to a large proportion of Soviet nuclear submarine forces and some strategic airfields.

The least glamorous, but most valuable of all, was SAC's RC-135 fleet. Again the aircraft were often tasked by USAFE, PACAF, and other US agencies to collect the highest national priority intelligence. Flown by 55th SRW crews, the rear compartment operators were drawn from the United States Air Force Security Service (USAFSS) (later Electronic Security Command). In northern Europe, work involved missions over the Barents Sea, the Baltic Sea, and along the inner German border. In southern Europe, missions from Greece and Crete covered the entire Mediterranean and into the Black Sea. Elsewhere, missions from Kadena AB in Japan and Alaska largely covered targets in the Soviet Far East and Pacific. Of special interest was the terminal missile target range at Klyuchi in Kamchatka. The early RC-135Cs and Ms concentrated on communications intelligence collection. Later, the specialist RC-135U "Combat Sent" variant was devoted to collecting electronic and radar emissions from aircraft, missile, and ground systems while its RC-135V "Rivet Joint" platforms specialized in collecting communications intelligence. Most missions either flew direct from Offutt AFB to target areas or from temporary duty bases at RAF Mildenhall, Athens (later Crete), Kadena in Japan, and Shemya in the Aleutian Islands to monitor Soviet missile tests.

To make a refueling join up, the KC-135Q orbited at 26,000ft and rolled out ahead of the approaching SR-71 flying at 25,000ft. (USAF)

100th ARW KC-135Qs carried the SR-71s special JP-7 fuel and equipment that gave the SR-71 the tankers' bearing and distance from up to 200 miles away. (USAF)

The KC-10As flying boom was more maneuverable for refueling SR-71s than the KC-135Q. (USAF, SSgt Ranzeno Oates)

An SR71A prepares for departure from RAF Mildenhall. It was a high-demand SAC asset especially with its high-resolution radar able to penetrate cloud. (USAF)

Rivet Joint RC-135Ws based at Offutt AFB, Nebraska, were regular visitors to Europe to operate over the Barents, Baltic, and Mediterranean Seas. (USAF/TSgt Scott Stewart)

Chapter 10

Command, Control, Communications

Good quality communications were vital for SAC's routine peacetime operations. In a crisis, they were critical. SAC operated worldwide voice and data radio networks and was an early user of digital data links and a leader in the development of data networks. It used a wide range of local, national, and international VHF and UHF radio nets and to give global coverage, made extensive use of high frequency radio and relay stations. These were used for routine clear communications and coded messages.

Often temperamental and dependent on weather conditions, in times of tension and war these communication networks were particularly vulnerable. Once the US developed a secure second-strike capability, reliable communications between its commanders, missile launch and bomber

By early 1961, new visual displays and large screens provided a wide range of operational data to aid SAC commanders' decision making. (USAF)

force controllers in post-attack scenarios were even more important. The Post-Attack Command and Control System (PACCS) evolved into a sophisticated network intended to remain viable in the most dire situations. A key role in its operation was played by SAC units and the US Navy with its Polaris and Trident submarine fleet. For two years EB-47s were interim PACCS aircraft, until the first EC-135s arrived in 1963.

The SAC Airborne Command Post, codenamed "Looking Glass," flying EC-135Cs from Offutt AFB became the central element of the system. This alternate command and control system overlapped with SAC's ground-based mechanisms able to link up with other USAF airborne command posts in Europe and the Pacific. The aircraft's communication fits gradually improved and the operation was supported by a dedicated air-refueling squadron of KC-135As. From 1970 to 1990, between 26 and 29 EC-135s were committed to the task at various times. A Looking Glass aircraft was continuously airborne from February 3, 1961, until July 24, 1990, each carrying an "airborne battle staff" of about 20, plus the aircrew and support staff.

The deployment of the Minuteman II from 1965 and the Titan II meant that as long as the missiles survived, buried deep in their silos across central and northern USA, some could be launched remotely by relaying Emergency Action Messages to them. However, the launch functions could not be easily combined with those of the Looking Glass EC-135Cs. To remote launch, more than one aircraft had to be within communication distance of the widely spaced Minuteman missile fields. Airfields at

The early 1960s Looking Glass Airborne Command Posts were considerably more primitive than later versions. (NARA)

A "Looking Glass" EC-135C airborne command and control aircraft arrives at Biggs Army Airfield, El Paso, TX, during exercise Busy Prairie II. (USAF/SSgt Bill Thompson)

The 28th BW's KC-135Rs operated mainly in support of the wing's 4th ACCS EC-135s. (USAF/TSgt Michael J Haggerty)

Gen Richard Ellis, SAC's commander aboard his EC-135C during Exercise *Global Shield '79*. (USAF/SSgt John Marine)

A 4th ACCS, 28th BW EC-135G overflies its home base in July 1988. (USAF/TSgt Michael Haggerty)

Ellsworth, South Dakota, and Minot, North Dakota, as well as Offutt, operated several EC-135A, C, and G variants as Airborne Launch Control Centers (ALCCs) and EC-135Ls as PACCS relay aircraft. The first test launch of a Minuteman missile from Vandenberg AB using an ALCC-configured aircraft took place on April 17, 1967. There was also an Emergency Rocket Communications System that could place a small UHF transmitter satellite into low Earth orbit from a Minuteman missile. This enabled the transmission of a recorded voice message and ALCC communications. It is difficult to overestimate the importance of the PACCS to the value of the nuclear deterrent, because it assured, despite weaknesses, a viable second-strike capability. As Robert Hopkins put it: "In the delicate nuclear balance of terror that defined the Cold War, PACCS ensured the odds were also even."

Above: **Capt Tom Neiss, a 2nd ACCS Launch Control Officer and his colleague Capt John Rogers, practice turning the missile launch keys inside their EC-135 aircraft prior to SAC's final Minuteman ICBM missile launch on March 22, 1991. (USAF/ SSgt Scott Stewart)**

Left: **A close-up view of the launch key station in 2nd ACCS EC-135C Looking Glass aircraft. Two launch control officers had to turn separate keys in order to transmit a launch order to the silo-housed Minuteman III missiles. (USAF/SSgt Scott Stewart)**

At Vandenberg AFB an EC-135 Airborne Launch Control Center prepares for a Minuteman test launch in August 1987. (USAF/SSgt Michael Best)

A flight over Mount Rushmore by the three aircraft types assigned to the 28th BW: B-1B, KC-135R, and EC-135C. (USAF/TSgt Michael Haggerty)

Even more secretive were the arrangements for ensuring presidential control of US nuclear forces and continuity of government in times of war. Early arrangements used three modified KC-135As as the first National Emergency Airborne Command Post (NEACP). Based at Andrews AFB, known as "Night Watch," it was to carry the president, key advisors, and a battle staff from February 1962. These were extremely basic and in March 1966 were replaced by three EC-135Js until the arrival of the Advanced Airborne Command Post (AABNCP) modified from a standard Boeing 747. Three aircraft were delivered to SAC in an interim E-4A configuration from 1974, with the fourth, now an E-4B, soon after. The other three airframes soon followed, being upgraded to E-4Bs. The aircraft were operated by the 1st Airborne Command and Control Squadron based at Offutt, with one E-4B at Andrews AFB, when the US president was in Washington, DC, and would shadow his movements around the US and overseas as necessary. A major weakness of the system was always assessing if the president would have sufficient time, or the will, to reach Andrews AFB in time to allow the E-4 to get clear of Washington, DC, in the face of a major attack. In such a situation, the president's place could have been taken by another member of the US National Command Authority such as the vice president or the Secretary for Defense.

An E-4B, known early on as "Night Watch," operated as presidential airborne command posts from which they could direct operations. (USAF/SSgt Michael Haggerty)

A night view of an E-4B at Osan AB in South Korea. The aircraft regularly accompanied US presidents on overseas trips. (USAF)

When in the US, an E-4B was constantly ready to get airborne with the president or another representative of the National Command Authority in an emergency. (USAF)

Chapter 11

Declining Cold War and Sudden Hot War

E uropean-based SAC nuclear operations were always a sensitive topic for the US, UK, and other
NATO member governments. While the B-52D's emphasis was on conventional weapon loads,
after its retirement in 1983, the B-52G/H models – which now undertook periodic European
deployments – were more likely to be "nuclear ready." Additional modifications allowed the G/H
models to more rapidly switch between nuclear and conventional roles, potentially changing the
European nuclear balance. Their dual-capable nature needs to be viewed in an early 1980s context,
when the Soviets were extremely nervous about NATO's nuclear modernization and the introduction
of land-based cruise missiles. The periodic arrival of SAC B-52s in Europe was of great concern to
Soviet military intelligence, and a significant "war indicator" for them.

An idea of this sensitivity is contained in declassified "after action" reports from the controversial
Able Archer '83 exercise. The event was regarded by many planners, and participants, as a "nuclear
weapons procedures exercise." Some were concerned that simply deploying significant numbers of SAC
"advanced echelon" personnel to Europe for the exercise could make the Soviets nervous. The inference
was that if SAC B-52s were taking part in a "nuclear procedures exercise," then their use was likely
to be in a nuclear role, even though for the exercise they were tasked to fly conventional attacks. In
subsequent years, SAC involvement in these exercises was significantly curtailed.

An Air Liaison Officer guides in a B-52 over the US Grafenwoehr range in West Germany during August 1988. (USAF/SSgt Michael Karlek)

A 2nd BW B-52G, part of a 1988 "Busy Brewer" deployment to the UK, drops retarded Mk 82 HE Bombs at low level over the Grafenwoehr range in Bavaria. (USAF/Sgt Tubridy)

A B-52 Stratofortress over the Egyptian desert during Exercise *Bright Star '83*. (US Joint Service Audiovisual Team)

A security policeman stands guard with an M16 rifle, while a munitions convoy delivers weapons to a B-52G during an ORI. Security personnel were vital to SAC, guarding its aircraft, bases, missile silos, weapons stores, and other facilities. (USAF/SSgt Phil Schmitten)

SAC and the 1991 Gulf War

Iraq's invasion of Kuwait in August 1990 saw the US mount Operation *Desert Shield* and aircraft, people, and material poured into the region. The Gulf was SAC's third and final "shooting war." Its B-52Gs became a major component of the coalition air forces, hurled against the Iraqis from January 17, 1991. B-52Gs flew just 3 per cent of the sorties in *Desert Storm*, but delivered 30 per cent of all the US ordnance dropped on Iraq. However, without its KC-10A and KC-135 tankers, the war could simply not have taken place at all.

As part of the opening wave of air strikes, 8th Air Force B-52s from the 2nd BW's, 596th Bomb Squadron CBS, used AGM-86 Conventional Air-l Launched Cruise MissileS (CALCMS) against high-value Iraqi targets. It was so secret that even the operation's official codename, *Senior Surprise*, was classified; crews unofficially re-christened it "Secret Squirrel." On January 16, 1991, just after 0600hrs, seven 596th BS B-52Gs launched in heavy drizzling rain and darkness from Barksdale AFB. General Shuler, now commander of SAC's Eighth Air Force oversaw the mission:

"We had placed one of my staff officers in each of the regional air traffic control centers along their route over the US, at Atlanta and Jacksonville. When our aircraft turned up on their radar, my guys tapped the controller on the shoulder and told him 'these aircraft are going to go from point A to B to C. Keep all traffic away from them and, by the way, they are not going to be talking to you.' They coasted out around Savannah, Georgia, and avoided commercial air routes. Crossing the Atlantic, they entered the Mediterranean over Gibraltar and soon after were intercepted by the Spanish Air Force. They came up and took a look at the airplanes, went away and nothing was ever said."

SAC KC-10As were key to deploying F-117As to Saudi Arabia during Operation *Desert Shield*. (USAF)

A now camouflaged KC-10A is guided into its parking space. During the Gulf War their dual refueling and cargo capacities were vital for early deployments to the Middle East. (USAF/SSgt Lono Kollars)

In February 1991, an RC135 Rivet Joint prepares to air refuel during *Desert Storm*. (USAF/TSgt Donald McMichael)

At Offutt AFB a K-loader carrying ammunition and other equipment transfers it to a waiting KC-135E during *Desert Shield*. (USAF/Sgt David Zubiate)

Two specially designed remote-control hydraulic trailers have uploaded two pylons, each fitted with six AGM-86B ALCMs, on to a B-52G. (USAF/SSgt Bob Simons)

A 92nd BW crew fit an ALCM pylon on to a B-52 during the SAC's 1985 Combat Weapons Loading Competition at Ellsworth AFB. (USAF/SSgt Rose Reynolds)

Above: A missile crew from the 416th BW transport a single ALCM for a B-52G at Griffiths AFB in 1981. (USAF/ TSgt Pablo Marmolejo)

Below left: A munitions maintenance crew works at night to secure a multiple AGM-86B ALCM pylon under the wing of a B-52G during a 1986 ORI at Barksdale AFB. (USAF/SSgt Phil Schmitten)

Below right: More ALCMs could be carried on a specialized rotary launcher fitted into the B-52s bomb bay. (USAF)

The B-52s refueled near the Azores and again over the Mediterranean.

"They flew well north of Libya; we did not want Gaddafi giving the Iraqis a tip-off. They overflew the eastern Mediterranean without a flight plan. I had told mission commander John Beard 'that no matter what happens, whoever calls you, just ignore it and press on.' They descended around the Red Sea, went to low level in trail formation, and launched their missiles in sequence. The rule was if the cruise missile did not check out perfectly before launch, it was to be retained and brought home."

In total, 35 CALCMS were successfully launched. "After rippling off their missiles, the crews retraced their steps and headed back homeward."

Above: On board the aircraft, SSgt Craig Van Wagenen works the ALCM panel on a B-52G in 1984. (USAF/SSgt Bob Simons)

Right: The opening B-52 ALCM strike of *Desert Storm* was so secret that even the code name was classified. The 2nd Bomb Wing crews quietly renamed it "Secret Squirrel" after the cartoon character from the 1960s. (USAF)

Moron AB in Spain was a vital location for SAC KC-10As, refueling aircraft transiting to the Middle East during the *Desert Shield* build-up and later refueling B-52s. (USAF/SSgt Louis Briscese)

"As they entered the Mediterranean again, they hit bad weather, but managed a difficult refueling with the KC-10s out of Moron. Into the Atlantic, headwinds of over 130kts were much higher than forecast. So we had to rush two more KC-10s out of Moron to fly west to catch up with the bombers for another refueling. They did a superb job." The bombers had flown, non-stop, over 14,000 miles and were airborne for over 35 hours–then the longest bombing mission in history.

B-52s in the Gulf War

During planning for the land war phase, General Norman Schwarzkopf insisted that before the ground assault, Iraqi Republican Guard positions should be hit every three hours. Air boss, General Charles Horner and USAF planners considered how to most effectively use the B-52 against the Iraqi troops. Such intensity required in-theater airbases, but these were scarce. Prince Abdullah AB, Jeddah, was one B-52-capable airfield, but the Saudi government did not allow it to be used until after the air campaign started. These aircraft, operating as the 1708 BW (Provisional), dropped half of all B-52 munitions released during the war. Other B-52s were stationed out of theater, where key planning factors included suitable runways, large fuel supplies, and access to the ordnance stocks necessary for extended operations.

Moron AB in Spain was nominated early on and later so was RAF Fairford in the UK. It possessed suitable airfield infrastructure to manage the heavyweight and was close to the RAF Welford US weapons store. However, its use for Gulf operations was only practical if the French government permitted the bombers to transit their airspace and that agreement only came 15 days after the main air assault had begun. Across the rest of Europe, B-52s were launched from Mont-de-Marsan in France and at Athens-Hellinikon, with tanker support flying out of Mont-de-Marsan and Milan Malpensa airport in Italy. Diego Garcia in the Indian Ocean had become a temporary B-52G base soon after US mobilization began in August 1990, but its distance from the Gulf placed it at the limit of practicality.

Loaded with M-117 bombs, B-52G *SAC Time* is prepared for a mission against Iraqi forces from King Abdulaziz Airport in Saudi Arabia. (USAF/Chester Falkenhainer)

A line-up of M-117-loaded B-52Gs operating with the 1708th BW (Provisional) at King Abdulaziz Airport in Saudi Arabia. (USAF/TSgt Rose Reynolds)

**Ground crew check a .50-caliber tail gun turret on a B-52G during Operation *Desert Shield*.
(USAF/Chief MSgt Don Sutherland)**

Almost all the B-52 missions after "Secret Squirrel" used "dumb" iron bombs. In a high-tech war of laser-guided smart bombs and cruise missiles, the B-52 bombing was a decidedly low-tech experience. While the B-52s were not counted upon for destroying equipment, they were the prime resource for attacking area targets, breaching defensive berms, minefields, ammunition stockpiles, troop concentrations, and field headquarters. Flying 1,741 sorties B-52s dropped 72,289 munitions, weighing 27,000 tons.

Above left and above right: 27 x 750lb M-117 bombs could be carried in the bomb bay of the B-52G, together with another 12 on each of the two underwing pylons. (USAF)

Chapter 12

Closing SAC, but Remaining Strategic

S AC's 13th and last commander was General George Lee Butler. He was a product of the SAC machine, having joined the USAF in 1961, and had accumulated more than 3,500 flying hours in C-141s, KC-135s, B-52s, B-1s, and F-4s. Following periods in staff appointments and as CO of two B-52 wings, he was assigned to SAC Headquarters as its IG in July 1984. As he said, "Two years later, I knew the command inside out."

By 1988–89 it was clear the Cold War was coming to an end, soon sealed by the conclusion of several arms control and reduction agreements with the USSR. Those at the top of US forces began to consider what the future strategic environment would look like. Soon after General Colin Powell became chair of the Joint Chiefs in 1989, Butler said, "We abandoned global war with the Soviet Union as the principal planning and programming paradigm for the US armed forces." In July 1989, Butler became the JCS Director for Strategic Plans and Policy (J-5) and explained that, "at the core, Strategic Air Command was a nuclear outfit, had always been, was, and would always be. I knew that unless that perception changed, the air assets that had traditionally been assigned to SAC would wither away and be lost. I could think of no other avenue to ensure that this did not happen than to recommend that SAC be disestablished and its assets reallocated." Subsequent JCS planning envisaged a major contraction of nuclear forces, with Butler heavily involved in the decisions to deactivate the Minuteman II force, stand down the B-52Gs, and withdraw 75 tankers.

Appointed SAC's last commander, he officially took post on January 25, 1991, just over a week into the opening phase of Operation *Desert Storm*. He was looking at "a command that was going to shrink at a minimum from 68 bases to 16." Following the 1991 Gulf War, Butler called a "lessons learned conference" to review SAC's performance in theater. Convinced that his new command had generally performed poorly (apart from the tankers), he was determined that SAC now had to adapt and develop more conventional capabilities or risk becoming sidelined in the post-Cold War world.

His remodeling of SAC envisaged it moving from "a nuclear command to a balanced nuclear and conventional-capable command." The B-52s were to be the key element capable of operating in both roles, as was the new B-2, just about to enter service. Butler's proposal was to disband SAC and form a much smaller "Strategic Command" to manage USAF and the US Navy's Trident missile submarines. In the vastly different strategic environment of the early 1990s, despite the natural disgruntlement within SAC, the opposition was muted. On June 1, 1992, as part of a wholesale reorganization of the USAF, SAC was disbanded and replaced by a new Strategic Command, again headed by General Butler until 1994.

SAC's existence had always been about nuclear weapons and its ability to deter and, if necessary, effectively use them. SAC's deterrent power was derived not just from its huge stock of nuclear weapons, but also from its capability to react rapidly. But this was only ever possible because of the people that operated, maintained, and supported its aircraft and missiles. The aircrews, aircraft

ADVANCED TECHNOLOGY BOMBER (ATB)

Well aware of the ageing SAC B-52 fleet, the Advanced Technology Bomber (ATB) was conceived as a black project in 1978. It was designed to incorporate the latest stealth technology, with Northrop as the main contractor by 1981. Very little reliable information about the ATB was released until 1988, when the first artist's illustrations emerged showing its "low observable" design characteristics. First flying in 1989, the obvious reductions in Cold War tensions saw the proposed purchase of the now-designated B-2 reduced from 132 airframes to just 21. The first was delivered to Whiteman AFB in December 1993 after SAC's formal demise.

Above: The roll-out of a B-2A from Plant 42 at Palmdale in November 1988. (USAF/MSgt Patrick Nugent)

Right: Northrop's chief test pilot Bruce Hinds and the USAF's Lt Col John Small fly a B-2 on a test flight in September 1989. (USAF)

Not quite as old as the pyramids, the B-52 first flew in April 1952 and retains its strategic role more than 70 years later. Here it is operating from Cairo West airport for a joint US–Egyptian training exercise, *Bright Star*, in July 1983. (USAF)

maintainers, missile launch crews, technicians, command post personnel, security police, and myriad others all had vital roles. Success depended on them all, many having awesome responsibilities at a very young age and often after just a few brief weeks of training. All this took place in international and domestic political contexts that were sometimes highly confrontational and sometimes seemed just a hair's breadth away from mass destruction.

Snapshots of SAC Bomber and Tanker Types and Strength

Year	B29	B50	KB29	B36	B47	KC97	B52	KC135	B58	FB111	KC10	B1	Total
1946	148												148
1950	286	196	126	38									646
1955			82	205	1086	679	18						2070
1960					1178	689	538	405	19				2826
1965					114		600	642	93				1449
1970							459	630		42			1131
1975							420	625		69			1114
1980							343	517		63			923
1985							261	506		60	39		866
1990							222	471		30	59	94	876

Source: *Alert Operations and SAC, 1957–91* (SAC: 1991)

Other books you might like:

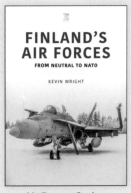

Air Forces Series,
Vol. 6

Air Forces Series,
Vol. 8

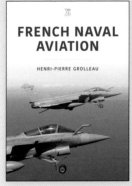

Modern Military Aircraft
Series, Vol. 7

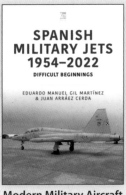

Modern Military Aircraft
Series, Vol. 9

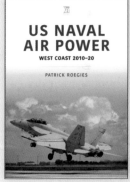

Air Forces Series,
Vol. 8

For our full range of titles please visit:
shop.keypublishing.com/books

VIP Book Club

Sign up today and receive
TWO FREE E-BOOKS

Be the first to find out about our forthcoming
book releases and receive exclusive offers.

Register now at keypublishing.com/vip-book-club

Our VIP Book Club is a 100% spam-free zone, and we will never share your email with anyone else.
You can read our full privacy policy at: privacy.keypublishing.com